BROADWAY SONGS FOR TWO

Arrangements by Peter Deneff

ISBN 978-1-5400-1288-3

HAL•LEONARD®

7777 W. BLUEMOUND RD. P.O. BOX 13819 MILWAUKEE, WI 53213

Visit Hal Leonard Online at
www.halleonard.com

CONTENTS

ANY DREAM WILL DO

from JOSEPH AND THE AMAZING TECHNICOLOR® DREAMCOAT

VIOLINS

Music by ANDREW LLOYD WEBBER
Lyrics by TIM RICE

BRING HIM HOME

from LES MISÉRABLES

VIOLINS

Music by CLAUDE-MICHEL SCHÖNBERG
Lyrics by HERBERT KRETZMER
and ALAIN BOUBLIL

Music and English Lyrics Copyright © 1986 by Alain Boublil Music Ltd. (ASCAP)
French Lyrics Copyright © 1991 by Éditions Musicales Alain Boublil
This edition Copyright © 2017 by Alain Boublil Music Ltd. (ASCAP)
Mechanical and Publication Rights for the U.S.A. Administered by Alain Boublil Music Ltd. (ASCAP) c/o Spielman Koenigsberg & Parker LLP,
Richard Koenigsberg, 1745 Broadway, New York NY 10019, Tel 212-453-2500, Fax 212-453-2550, ABML@skpny.com
International Copyright Secured. All Rights Reserved. This music is copyright. Photocopying is illegal.
All Performance Rights Restricted.

CABARET
from the Musical CABARET

VIOLINS

Words by FRED EBB
Music by JOHN KANDER

EDELWEISS
from THE SOUND OF MUSIC

VIOLINS

Lyrics by OSCAR HAMMERSTEIN II
Music by RICHARD RODGERS

FOR FOREVER

from DEAR EVAN HANSEN

VIOLINS

Music and Lyrics by BENJ PASEK
and JUSTIN PAUL

HELLO, DOLLY!

from HELLO, DOLLY!

VIOLINS

Music and Lyric by
JERRY HERMAN

I BELIEVE

from the Broadway Musical THE BOOK OF MORMON

VIOLINS

Words and Music by TREY PARKER,
ROBERT LOPEZ and MATT STONE

I WHISTLE A HAPPY TUNE

from THE KING AND I

VIOLINS

Lyrics by OSCAR HAMMERSTEIN II
Music by RICHARD RODGERS

IF I WERE A BELL

from GUYS AND DOLLS

VIOLINS

By FRANK LOESSER

THE IMPOSSIBLE DREAM

(The Quest)

from MAN OF LA MANCHA

VIOLINS

Lyric by JOE DARION
Music by MITCH LEIGH

MAMMA MIA
from MAMMA MIA!

VIOLINS

Words and Music by BENNY ANDERSSON,
BJÖRN ULVAEUS and STIG ANDERSON

MEMORY
from CATS

VIOLINS

Music by ANDREW LLOYD WEBBER
Text by TREVOR NUNN after T.S. ELIOT

Slowly, with feeling

MY FAVORITE THINGS
from THE SOUND OF MUSIC

VIOLINS

Lyrics by OSCAR HAMMERSTEIN II
Music by RICHARD RODGERS

ONE

from A CHORUS LINE

Music by MARVIN HAMLISCH
Lyric by EDWARD KLEBAN

VIOLINS

POPULAR

from the Broadway Musical WICKED

VIOLINS

Music and Lyrics by
STEPHEN SCHWARTZ

SEASONS OF LOVE

from RENT

VIOLINS

Words and Music by
JONATHAN LARSON

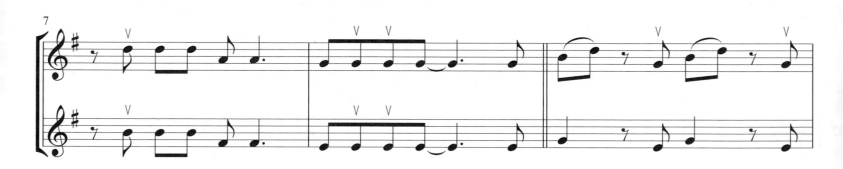

SEVENTY SIX TROMBONES

from Meredith Willson's THE MUSIC MAN

VIOLINS

By MEREDITH WILLSON

SUMMERTIME
from PORGY AND BESS®

VIOLINS

Music and Lyrics by GEORGE GERSHWIN,
DuBOSE and DOROTHY HEYWARD
and IRA GERSHWIN

SUNRISE, SUNSET

from the Musical FIDDLER ON THE ROOF

VIOLINS

Words by SHELDON HARNICK
Music by JERRY BOCK

TOMORROW
from the Musical Production ANNIE

VIOLINS

Lyric by MARTIN CHARNIN
Music by CHARLES STROUSE

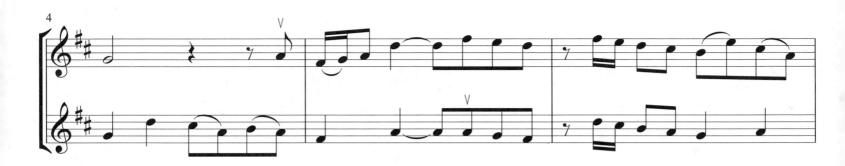

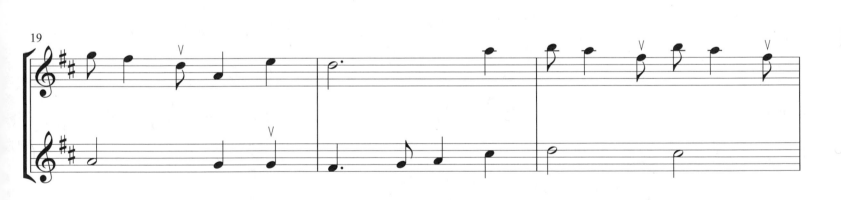

WHERE IS LOVE?

from the Broadway Musical OLIVER!

VIOLINS

Words and Music by
LIONEL BART

YOU'VE GOT A FRIEND

featured in BEAUTIFUL: THE CAROLE KING MUSICAL

VIOLINS

Words and Music by
CAROLE KING

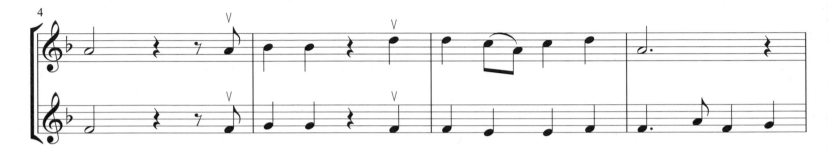

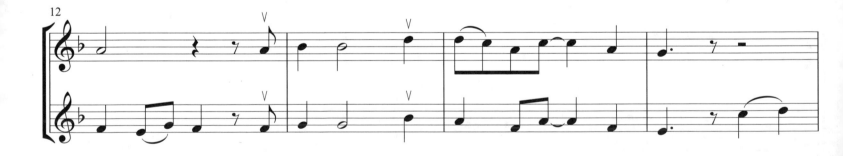